barbecue

TRADITIONAL AND MODERN RECIPES
FOR A SUMMER BARBECUE

LINDA DOESER

MAIN PHOTOGRAPHY BY IAN PARSONS

This is a Parragon Publishing Book
This edition published in 2004

Parragon Publishing
Queen Street House
4 Queen Street
Bath BA1 1HE, UK

Created and produced for Parragon by The Bridgewater Book Company Ltd.

Home economists Sara Hesketh and Richard Green
Additional photography Calvey Taylor-Haw (10, 34, 46, 54, 94)

ISBN: 1-40540-628-3

Printed in China

NOTE

*This book uses imperial and metric measurements. Follow the same units of
measurement throughout; do not mix imperial and metric. All spoon measurements
are level: teaspoons are assumed to be 5 ml and tablespoons are assumed to be 15 ml.
Unless otherwise stated, milk is assumed to be whole milk, eggs and individual vegetables
such as potatoes are medium, and pepper is freshly ground black pepper.*

*The times given for each recipe are an approximate guide only because the preparation
times may differ according to the techniques used by different people and the cooking times may
vary as a result of the type of oven used. Ovens should be preheated to the specified temperature.
If using a fan-assisted oven, check the manufacturer's instructions for adjusting the time and
temperature. The preparation times include chilling and marinating times, where appropriate.*

*Recipes using raw or very lightly cooked eggs should be avoided by infants, the elderly,
pregnant women, convalescents, and anyone suffering from an illness.*

Contents

Introduction

Cooking food outdoors on a barbecue is great fun and a delicious way of feeding a crowd. To keep everybody happy, it is always a good idea to offer a range of meat and seafood dishes, vegetables, salads, and desserts, so there is something for meat-eaters, vegetarians, and even fussy children.

The dishes can be as straightforward or complicated as you wish. You can start by

cooking a basic barbecue with traditional ingredients such as burgers, chicken drumsticks, chops, steaks, and sausages. Served with burger buns, French bread or baked potatoes, and plenty of fresh leafy or mixed salad, good food doesn't get much easier.

Once you have got the hang of cooking on your grill, you can experiment with more elaborate dishes. Thread seafood, poultry, vegetables, or fruit on to wooden skewers to make kabobs. Add extra flavor and succulence to the food by mixing various marinades and dressings.

The key to a successful barbecue is good planning. It helps to know roughly how many people are coming. If the numbers are very vague or large, you need to lay on a plentiful supply of

basics, such as burgers, salad, and bread, so that nobody goes hungry. Reserve supplies can be kept in the refrigerator and frozen later if not needed.

To cater for vegetarian guests, prepare plenty of vegetable kabobs and pockets which others can eat too. Offer different fillings to go with baked potatoes: a creamy cheese or a spicy corn relish are very popular. A good selection of colorful salads, including a pasta, rice, tomato, or mixed bean salad, will please vegetarians and appeal to everyone else as well.

Safety

Grilling is a safe way of cooking as long as you take a few sensible precautions.

• Position your grill away from overhanging trees and shrubs to avoid branches catching fire. Have a bucket of water nearby in case the fire blows out of control.

• Trim off excess fat and shake away surplus

marinade before putting the food on the grill to stop fat dripping down on to the hot coals and bursting into flames.

• To minimize the risk of food poisoning, make sure that meat and seafood are cooked through. Test the meat by piercing it with a skewer or the tip of a sharp knife—it is cooked when the juices run clear (not pink). Once poultry has cooled down, never return it to the grill to finish cooking.

• Keep salads and cooked foods away from raw meat. Use different chopping boards, utensils, dish towels, and plates for dealing with raw and cooked meats or salad ingredients.

• On hot days, store foods out of direct sunlight and keep them chilled for as long as possible before cooking or serving. Cover food with netting or clean dish towels to keep insects off.

• Never leave the grill unattended. Warn any small children to keep away from the hot fire. Ban pets from the food and cooking areas as well, to prevent contamination and accidents.

• Use long-handled utensils and oven gloves to avoid getting burned and splashed.

• The person cooking should go easy on the alcohol, as a drunken cook can be a dangerous one. Discourage other adults who also have been drinking from cooking.

Equipment

There are many different types of fuel on the market, and an equally wide range of grills, so you should consider your exact requirements before spending any money.

Types of fuel

First, decide on the fuel you want to use first:

● Lumpwood charcoal is readily available, inexpensive, and easy to light, but burns quickly.

● Charcoal briquettes take longer to catch, but burn for a long time and produce little smoke.

● Self-igniting charcoal is lumpwood charcoal or charcoal briquettes that have been coated with a flammable chemical. They light easily but you cannot start cooking until the chemical has burnt off as it can taint the food.

● Wood fires need constant attention. Hardwoods, such as mesquite, oak, and apple, are best as they burn slowly and have a pleasant smell. Softwoods burn too fast and tend to spark.

● Wood chips and herbs, such as sprigs of thyme or rosemary, can be sprinkled on the fire to give off a delicious aroma.

Choosing your grill

Before buying a grill, consider the number of people you will want to feed; how often you are likely to use it; how it will fit into your yard; and how much you are prepared to spend on it.

● Disposable grills are inexpensive foil trays with enough fuel to burn for about one hour—ideal for a small, one-off picnic.

● Hibachi or "firebox" grills from Japan are small, lightweight, reusable, and easy to transport.

● Portable grills are light and easy to fold up and carry in the trunk of a car for larger picnics.

● Brazier grills can be moved about the yard and stored easily. Some are a little low so check that the one you are thinking of buying is a comfortable height for the person who will be doing most of the cooking. If your yard is windy, choose one with a hood to protect the open grill.

● Kettle-grills are the next best thing to a permanent grill. The lid covers the grill and can save a barbecue party if it starts to rain. Many have a rotisserie for cooking chickens and joints.

● Gas and electric grills are expensive but easy to operate and very quick—they only take ten minutes to warm up. However, they do not give the food the traditional smoky flavor it gets from being cooked over charcoal.

● Permanent, tailor-made grills are an excellent choice if you grill frequently. You can buy kits or use simple materials such as house- and fire-bricks to build a fireplace and fit an adjustable metal rack.

Preparation

It is possible to make some dishes for your grill, such as burgers and meat kabobs, well in advance and freeze them. Then all you have to do is remember to take them out the night before and thaw them thoroughly before cooking. Alternatively, you can make them the previous day and store them in the refrigerator overnight. You may also start marinating food the day before.

Leave the chopping and mixing of any salad ingredients until the morning of the barbecue. Toss in the dressing just before you are ready to serve them, so that the leaves and other ingredients do not go limp and soggy.

Hints and tips

- Remember to light your grill at least an hour before you want to start cooking to make sure it will be hot. For setting the fire, follow the instructions that come with the fuel you are using.
- To ensure even and thorough cooking, do not place too much food on the grill rack at once.
- Aim to cook the same types of food together to avoid contamination. Do not mix meat, fish, and vegetarian dishes on the grill. The best plan is to wrap the vegetarian ingredients in foil pockets.
- Foil-wrapped potatoes cook well, especially if you bake them in a conventional oven at 400°F/200°C for 30 minutes before moving them to the grill to finish cooking.
- Foil pockets are often the best solution for hot desserts. Just wrap the fruit and leave it to cook around the edge of the grill where the temperature is slightly lower.
- Offer a choice of drinks, both alcoholic and non-alcoholic: a fruit punch is usually popular.
- Even when rained out, you can keep cooking if you shut the lid of your grill and open the vents. Alternatively, you can take the food inside and carry on cooking under the broiler in your kitchen. When the sun appears again you can move back outside.

Meat
& Poultry

Tabasco Steaks with Parsley Butter

A variation on a classic theme, this simple, but rather extravagant dish would be ideal for a special occasion barbecue party.

serves 4

1 bunch of parsley

6 tbsp unsalted butter, softened

4 sirloin steaks, about 8 oz/225 g each

4 tsp Tabasco sauce

salt and pepper

Method

❶ Preheat the grill. Using a sharp knife, finely chop enough parsley to fill 4 tablespoons. Reserve a few parsley leaves for the garnish. Place the butter in a small bowl and beat in the chopped parsley with a fork until fully incorporated. Cover with plastic wrap and leave to chill in the refrigerator until required.

❷ Sprinkle each steak with 1 teaspoon of the Tabasco sauce, rubbing it in well. Season to taste with salt and pepper.

❸ Cook the steaks over hot coals: 2½ minutes each side for rare, 4 minutes each side for medium, and 6 minutes each side for well done. Transfer to serving plates, garnish with the reserved parsley leaves, and serve immediately, topped with the parsley butter.

Variation

If you can find watercress, substitute for the same amount of fresh parsley, if you prefer.

Best Ever Burgers

Barbecues and burgers are almost inseparable. However, these succulent, homemade burgers bear no resemblance to the little ready-made patties available in most stores.

serves 6

2 lb/900 g lean ground chuck	To serve
2 onions, finely chopped	6 sesame seed hamburger buns
½ cup fresh white bread crumbs	2 tomatoes
1 egg, lightly beaten	1 onion
1½ teaspoons finely chopped	lettuce leaves
fresh thyme	mayonnaise
salt and pepper	mustard
	tomato ketchup

Method

❶ Preheat the grill. Place the meat, onions, bread crumbs, egg, and thyme in a large glass bowl and season to taste with salt and pepper. Mix thoroughly using your hands.

❷ Form the mixture into 6 large burgers with your hands, neatening the edges with a round-bladed knife.

❸ Cook the burgers over hot coals for 3–4 minutes on each side. Meanwhile, cut the buns in half and briefly toast on the grill, cut-side down. Using a sharp knife, slice the tomatoes and cut the onion into thinly sliced rings. Fill the toasted buns with the cooked burgers, lettuce, sliced tomatoes, and onion rings and serve immediately, with the mayonnaise, mustard, and tomato ketchup.

Variation

For Tex-Mex burgers, add 2 seeded and finely chopped fresh green chiles to the mixture in Step 1 and serve with guacamole.

Luxury Cheeseburgers

This is a sophisticated version of the traditional burger with a surprise filling of melted blue cheese. Serve with plenty of salad to make a substantial barbecue lunch.

serves 4

2 oz/55 g Stilton cheese

1 lb/450 g lean ground chuck

1 onion, finely chopped

1 celery stalk, finely chopped

1 tsp creamed horseradish

1 tbsp chopped fresh thyme

salt and pepper

To serve

4 sesame seed hamburger buns

lettuce leaves

sliced tomatoes

Method

❶ Preheat the grill. Crumble the Stilton cheese into a bowl and reserve until required. Place the steak, onion, celery, horseradish, and thyme in a separate bowl and season to taste with salt and pepper. Mix thoroughly using your hands.

❷ Form the mixture into 8 burgers with your hands and a round-bladed knife. Divide the cheese between 4 of them and top with the remaining burgers. Gently press them together and mold the edges.

❸ Cook the burgers over hot coals for 5 minutes on each side. Meanwhile, cut the buns in half and briefly toast on the grill, cut-side down. Fill the buns with the cooked burgers, lettuce, and tomato slices and serve immediately.

Variation

Substitute Saga blue, Cheddar, or Swiss cheese for the Stilton cheese and finely snipped chives for the thyme.

Rack & Ruin

This quick and easy dish is perfect for serving as part of a summer party menu, along with plenty of salad and potatoes.

serves 4

4 racks of lamb, each with 4 rib chops	3 tbsp finely chopped fresh rosemary
2 tbsp extra virgin olive oil	1 small onion, finely chopped
1 tbsp balsamic vinegar	salt and pepper
1 tbsp lemon juice	

Method

❶ Place the racks of lamb in a large, shallow, nonmetallic dish. Make a marinade by placing the oil, vinegar, lemon juice, rosemary, and onion in a pitcher and stirring together. Season to taste with salt and pepper.

❷ Pour the marinade over the lamb and turn until thoroughly coated. Cover with plastic wrap. Marinate in the refrigerator for 1 hour, turning occasionally.

❸ Preheat the grill. Drain the racks of lamb, reserving the marinade. Cook over medium-hot coals, brushing frequently with the marinade, for 10 minutes on each side. Serve immediately.

Minted Lamb Steaks

You can prepare this dish with any kind of lamb chops—leg chops are especially tender—or rib chops, in which case you will probably require two per serving. Shoulder steaks also work well.

serves 6

6 sirloin chops, about 6 oz/175 g each

5 fl oz/150 ml natural Greek yogurt

2 garlic cloves, finely chopped

1 tsp grated fresh gingerroot

¼ tsp coriander seeds, crushed

salt and pepper

1 tbsp olive oil, plus extra for brushing

1 tbsp orange juice

1 tsp walnut oil

2 tbsp chopped fresh mint

Method

❶ Place the chops in a large, shallow, nonmetallic bowl. Mix half the yogurt, the garlic, ginger, and coriander seeds together in a pitcher and season to taste with salt and pepper. Spoon the mixture over the chops, turning to coat them evenly, then cover with plastic wrap and leave to marinate in the refrigerator for 2 hours, turning occasionally.

❷ Preheat the grill. Place the remaining yogurt, the olive oil, orange juice, walnut oil, and mint in a small bowl and, using a hand-held whisk, whisk until thoroughly blended. Season to taste with salt and pepper. Cover the minted yogurt with plastic wrap and leave to chill in the refrigerator until ready to serve.

❸ Drain the chops, scraping off the marinade. Brush with olive oil and cook over medium-hot coals for 5–7 minutes on each side. Serve immediately with the minted yogurt.

Variation

If you like, omit the orange juice and walnut oil and stir in ¼ teaspoon ground star anise and a pinch each of ground cinnamon and ground cumin.

Normandy Brochettes

The orchards of Normandy are famous throughout France, providing both eating apples and cider-making varieties. For an authentic touch, enjoy a glass of Calvados between courses.

serves 4

1 lb/450 g pork tenderloin	6 black peppercorns, crushed
1¼ cups hard cider	2 crisp eating apples
1 tbsp finely chopped fresh sage	1 tbsp sunflower oil

Method

❶ Using a sharp knife, cut the pork into 1-inch/2.5-cm cubes, then place in a large, shallow, nonmetallic dish. Mix the cider, sage, and peppercorns together in a pitcher, pour the mixture over the pork and turn until thoroughly coated. Cover with plastic wrap and leave to marinate in the refrigerator for 1–2 hours.

❷ Preheat the grill. Drain the pork, reserving the marinade. Core the apples, but do not peel, then cut into wedges. Dip the apple wedges into the reserved marinade and thread on to several flat, metal skewers, alternating with the cubes of pork. Stir the sunflower oil into the remaining marinade.

❸ Cook the brochettes over medium-hot coals, turning and brushing frequently with the reserved marinade, for 12–15 minutes. Transfer to a large serving plate and, if you prefer, remove the meat and apples from the skewers before serving. Serve immediately.

Variation

Replace 1 apple with 6 no-soak dried pitted prunes wrapped in strips of bacon. Thread the prunes on to the skewers with the remaining apple and pork.

Sausages with Barbecue Sauce

Although there is much more to barbecues than sausages, they can make a welcome appearance from time to time. This delicious sauce is a wonderful excuse for including them again.

serves 4

2 tbsp sunflower oil	4 tbsp white wine vinegar
1 large onion, chopped	½ tsp mild chili powder
2 cloves garlic, chopped	¼ tsp mustard powder
1 cup canned chopped tomatoes	dash of Tabasco sauce
1 tbsp Worcestershire sauce	1 lb/450 g sausages
2 tbsp brown fruity sauce	salt and pepper
2 tbsp light muscovado sugar	bread finger rolls, to serve

Method

❶ To make the sauce, heat the oil in a small pan and fry the onion and garlic for 4–5 minutes until softened and just beginning to brown.

❷ Add the tomatoes, Worcestershire sauce, brown fruity sauce, sugar, white wine vinegar, chili powder, mustard powder, and Tabasco sauce to the pan. Add salt and pepper to taste, and bring to a boil.

❸ Reduce the heat and simmer gently for 10–15 minutes until the sauce begins to thicken slightly. Stir occasionally so that the sauce does not burn and stick to the bottom of the pan. Set aside and keep warm until required.

❹ Preheat the barbecue. Grill the sausages over hot coals for 10–15 minutes, turning frequently. Do not prick them with a fork or the juices and fat will run out and cause the grill to flare.

❺ Insert the sausages into the bread rolls and serve with the barbecue sauce.

Variation

Choose any tasty "country" sausages for this recipe. Also try chorizo, frankfurter, Italian, and Toulouse sausages.

Meatballs on Sticks

These are popular with children and adults alike. Serve with a selection of
ready-made or homemade sauces, such as a tomato relish,
heated on the side of the grill.

serves 8

4 pork and herb sausages

4 oz/115 g ground beef

1½ cups fresh white bread crumbs

1 onion, finely chopped

2 tbsp chopped mixed fresh herbs,
such as parsley, thyme, and sage

1 egg

salt and pepper

sunflower oil, for brushing

sauces of your choice, to serve

Method

❶ Preheat the grill. Remove the sausage
meat from the skins, place in a large bowl,
and break up with a fork. Add the ground
beef, bread crumbs, onion, herbs, and egg.
Season to taste with salt and pepper
and stir well with a wooden spoon until
thoroughly mixed.

❷ Form the mixture into small balls, about
the size of a golf ball, between the palms
of your hands. Spear each one with a
wooden toothpick and brush with oil.

❸ Cook over medium–hot coals, turning
frequently and brushing with more oil as
necessary, for 10 minutes or until cooked
through. Transfer to a large serving plate
and serve immediately with a choice of
warmed sauces.

Variation

*Substitute 1 cooked potato and 1 cooked small
beet, both finely chopped, for the bread crumbs.*

Bacon Koftas

Koftas—molded kabobs—are usually made from a spicy mixture of ground lamb. These ones are economically based on lean bacon. While they are very easy to make, be careful not to over-process them.

serves 4

1 small onion

8 oz/225 g lean bacon, rinded and roughly chopped

1½ cups fresh white bread crumbs

1 tbsp chopped fresh marjoram

grated rind of 1 lemon

1 egg white

pepper

chopped nuts, for coating (optional)

paprika, to dust

snipped fresh chives, to garnish

Method

❶ Preheat the grill. Using a sharp knife, chop the onion, then put it into a food processor with the bacon, bread crumbs, marjoram, lemon rind, and egg white. Season to taste with pepper and process briefly, just until the mixture is blended.

❷ Divide the bacon mixture into 8 equal portions and form each around a skewer into a fat sausage. Dust the skewered koftas with paprika. If you like, form 4 of the portions into rounds rather than sausages, then spread the chopped nuts out on a large, flat plate and roll the rounds in them to coat.

❸ Cook over hot coals for 10 minutes, turning frequently. Transfer to a large serving plate and serve immediately, garnished with snipped fresh chives.

Fabulous Frankfurter Skewers

A new way with an old favorite—cook frankfurter sausages on the grill for a wonderful smoky flavor and an incredibly easy meal. They are served here with garlic toast.

serves 4

12 frankfurter sausages	Garlic toast
2 zucchini, cut into ½-inch/1-cm slices	2 garlic bulbs
2 corn cobs, cut into ½-inch/1-cm slices	2–3 tbsp olive oil
12 cherry tomatoes	1 baguette, sliced
12 baby onions	salt and pepper
2 tbsp olive oil	

Method

❶ Preheat the grill. To make the garlic toast, slice off the tops of the garlic bulbs. Brush the bulbs with oil and wrap them in foil. Cook over hot coals, turning occasionally, for 30 minutes.

❷ Meanwhile, cut each of the frankfurter sausages into 3 pieces. Thread the frankfurter pieces, zucchini slices, corn cob slices, cherry tomatoes, and baby onions alternately on to flat metal skewers. Brush with olive oil.

❸ Cook the skewers over hot coals, turning and brushing frequently with the oil, for 8–10 minutes. Meanwhile, brush the slices of baguette with oil and toast both sides on the grill. Unwrap the garlic bulbs and squeeze the cloves on to the bread. Season to taste with salt and pepper and drizzle over a little extra olive oil, if you like. Transfer the skewers to a large serving plate and serve immediately with the garlic toast.

Variation

Slice a baguette without cutting it right through. Spread with 2 crushed garlic cloves beaten into 4 oz/115 g butter. Wrap in foil and cook for 15 minutes.

Mustard & Honey Drumsticks

Chicken can taste rather bland, but this sweet-and-sour glaze gives it a wonderful piquancy and helps to keep it moist during cooking.

serves 4

8 chicken drumsticks	Glaze
fresh parsley sprigs, to garnish	4 fl oz/125 ml clear honey
salad, to serve	4 tbsp Dijon mustard
	4 tbsp wholegrain mustard
	4 tbsp white wine vinegar
	2 tbsp sunflower oil
	salt and pepper

Method

❶ Using a sharp knife, make 2–3 diagonal slashes in the chicken drumsticks and place them in a large, nonmetallic dish.

❷ Mix all the ingredients for the glaze together in a pitcher and season to taste with salt and pepper. Pour the glaze over the drumsticks, turning until the drumsticks are well coated. Cover with plastic wrap and leave to marinate in the refrigerator for at least 1 hour.

❸ Preheat the grill. Drain the chicken drumsticks, reserving the marinade. Cook the chicken over medium-hot coals, turning frequently and brushing with the reserved marinade, for 25–30 minutes, or until thoroughly cooked. Transfer to serving plates, garnish with fresh parsley sprigs, and serve immediately with salad.

Variation

Try this glaze with pork spareribs. Marinate 2 lb/900 g spare ribs in the glaze for 1 hour. Cook over hot coals, turning frequently and brushing with the glaze, for 15–20 minutes.

Sage & Lemon Squab Chickens

Spatchcocked squab chickens are the ideal choice for a barbecue, as they are easy to handle and look attractive.

serves 4

4 squab chickens, about 1 lb/450 g each

1 lemon

2 tbsp chopped fresh sage

salt and pepper

To garnish

fresh herb sprigs

lemon slices

Method

❶ Preheat the grill. To spatchcock the squab chickens, turn 1 bird breast-side down and, using strong kitchen scissors or poultry shears, cut through the skin and ribcage along both sides of the backbone, from tail to neck. Remove the backbone and turn the bird breast-side up. Press down firmly on the breastbone with the heel of your hand to flatten. Fold the wingtips underneath. Repeat with the remaining squab chickens.

❷ Thinly slice half the lemon and finely grate the rind of the other half. Mix the lemon rind and sage together in a small bowl. Loosen the skin over the breasts and legs of the squab chickens and insert the lemon and sage mixture. Tuck in the lemon slices and smooth the skin back firmly. Push a flat metal skewer into one wing, through the top of the breast, and out of the other wing. Push a second skewer into one thigh, through the bottom of the breast, and out of the other thigh. Season to taste with salt and pepper.

❸ Cook the squab chickens over medium-hot coals for 10–15 minutes on each side. Serve immediately, garnished with fresh herb sprigs and lemon slices.

Hot Red Chicken

Chicken pieces are used in this adaptation of a traditional Indian recipe for spring chickens, but you could substitute spatchcocked squab chickens if you prefer.

serves 4

1 tbsp curry paste

1 tbsp tomato ketchup

1 tsp Indian five-spice powder

1 fresh red chile, seeded and
finely chopped

1 tsp Worcestershire sauce

1 tsp sugar

salt

8 skinless chicken pieces

vegetable oil, for brushing

naan bread, to serve

To garnish

lemon wedges

fresh cilantro sprigs

Method

❶ Place the curry paste, tomato ketchup, five-spice powder, chile, Worcestershire sauce, and sugar in a small bowl, and stir until the sugar has dissolved. Season to taste with salt.

❷ Place the chicken pieces in a large, shallow, nonmetallic dish and spoon the spice paste over them, rubbing it in well. Cover with plastic wrap and leave to marinate in the refrigerator for up to 8 hours.

❸ Preheat the grill. Remove the chicken from the spice paste, discarding any remaining paste, and brush with oil. Cook the chicken over medium-hot coals, turning occasionally, for 25–30 minutes. Briefly heat the naan bread on the grill and serve with the chicken, garnished with lemon wedges and cilantro sprigs.

Turkey Rolls

These herb-flavored rolls conceal a soft center of melted cheese as a lovely surprise. They are served here with red currant relish, but would also be delicious with a mild mustard sauce.

serves 4

2 tbsp sunflower oil

salt and pepper

4 tbsp chopped fresh marjoram

4 turkey breast steaks

4 tsp mild mustard

6 oz/175 g Emmental cheese, grated

1 leek, thinly sliced

Relish

4 oz/115 g red currants

2 tbsp chopped fresh mint

2 tsp clear honey

1 tsp red wine vinegar

Method

❶ Preheat the grill. To make the red currant relish, place all the ingredients in a bowl and mash well with a fork. Season to taste with salt and pepper. Cover with plastic wrap and leave to chill in the refrigerator until required.

❷ Pour the oil into a small bowl, season to taste with pepper, and stir in 2 teaspoons of the marjoram. Reserve. Place the turkey steaks between 2 sheets of plastic wrap and beat with the side of a rolling pin to flatten. Season with salt and pepper and spread the mustard evenly over them. Divide the Emmental cheese, leek, and remaining marjoram between the turkey steaks, roll up, and tie securely with kitchen string.

❸ Brush the turkey rolls with the flavored oil and cook over medium-hot coals, turning and brushing frequently with the remaining oil, for 30 minutes. Serve immediately with the relish.

Variation

The red currant relish can be replaced with cranberry relish if preferred.

Tarragon Turkey

This economical dish is quick and simple to prepare, and yet it tastes absolutely wonderful, not least because poultry and tarragon have a natural affinity.

serves 4

4 turkey breast steaks,
about 6 oz/175 g each

salt and pepper

4 tsp wholegrain mustard

8 fresh tarragon sprigs,
plus extra to garnish

4 slices back bacon

salad greens, to serve

Method

❶ Preheat the grill. Season the turkey to taste with salt and pepper and, using a round-bladed knife, spread the mustard evenly over the turkey.

❷ Place 2 tarragon sprigs on top of each turkey breast and wrap a bacon slice around to hold the herbs in place. Secure with a wooden toothpick.

❸ Cook the turkey over medium-hot coals for 5–8 minutes on each side. Transfer to serving plates and garnish with tarragon sprigs. Serve with salad greens.

Fruity Duck

Apricots and onions counteract the richness of the duck. Its high fat content makes it virtually self-basting, so it stays superbly moist. The duck looks particularly elegant garnished with scallion tassels.

serves 4

4 duck breasts

4 oz/115 g ready-to-eat dried apricots

2 shallots, thinly sliced

2 tbsp clear honey

1 tsp sesame oil

2 tsp Chinese five-spice powder

4 scallions, to garnish

Method

❶ Preheat the grill. Using a sharp knife, cut a long slit in the fleshy side of each duck breast to make a pocket. Divide the apricots and shallots between the pockets and secure with skewers.

❷ Mix the honey and sesame oil together in a small bowl and brush all over the duck. Sprinkle with the five-spice powder. To make the garnish, make a few cuts lengthwise down the stem of each scallion. Place in a bowl of ice-cold water and leave until the tassels open out. Drain well before using.

❸ Cook the duck over medium-hot coals for 6–8 minutes on each side. Remove the skewers, transfer to a large serving plate, and garnish with the scallion tassels. Serve immediately.

Variation

Substitute 4 pork chops for the duck and cook over medium-hot coals for 8–9 minutes on each side, or until thoroughly cooked.

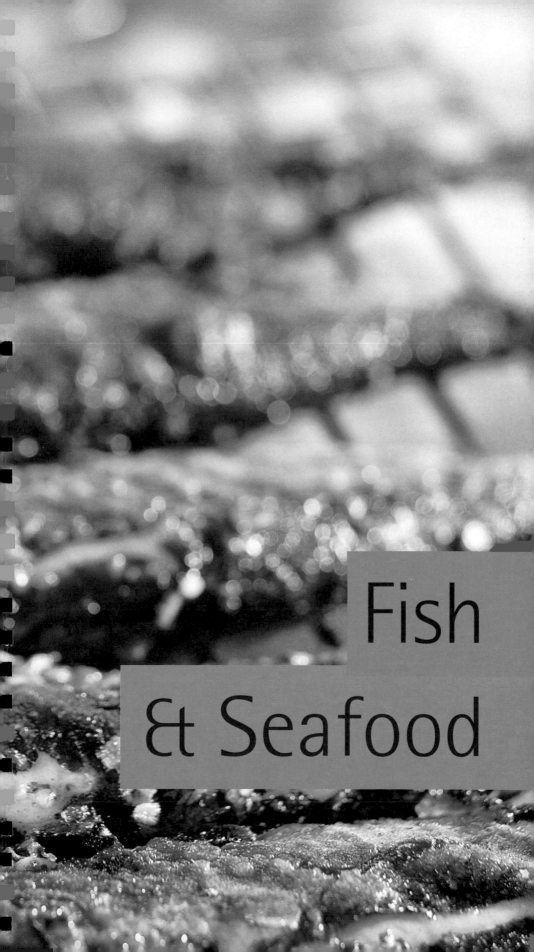

Fish
& Seafood

Caribbean Fish Kabobs

Lightly spiced and marinated, these colorful kabobs look and taste delicious.
You can use any firm-textured fish, but for an authentic Caribbean flavor,
swordfish is perfect.

serves 6

2 lb 4 oz/1 kg swordfish steaks

3 tbsp olive oil

3 tbsp lime juice

1 garlic clove, finely chopped

1 tsp paprika

salt and pepper

3 onions, cut into wedges

6 tomatoes, cut into wedges

Method

❶ Using a sharp knife, cut the fish into 1-inch/2.5-cm cubes and place in a shallow, nonmetallic dish. Place the oil, lime juice, garlic, and paprika in a pitcher and mix well. Season to taste with salt and pepper. Pour the marinade over the fish, turning to coat evenly. Cover with plastic wrap and leave to marinate in the refrigerator for 1 hour.

❷ Preheat the grill. Thread the fish cubes, onion wedges, and tomato wedges alternately on to 6 long, presoaked wooden skewers. Reserve the marinade.

❸ Cook the kabobs over medium-hot coals for 8–10 minutes, turning and brushing frequently with the reserved marinade. When they are cooked through, transfer the kabobs to a large serving plate and serve immediately.

Variation

Instead of serving the kabobs with traditional baked potatoes, serve them with baked sweet potatoes.

Salmon with Mango Salsa

Although an oily fish, salmon can dry out easily on the fierce heat of the grill. Make sure that it is well coated with the citrus juice before you begin cooking.

serves 4

4 salmon steaks, about 6 oz/175 g each

finely grated rind and juice

of 1 lime or ½ lemon

salt and pepper

Salsa

1 large mango, peeled,

pitted and diced

1 red onion, finely chopped

2 passion fruit

2 fresh basil sprigs

2 tbsp lime juice

salt

Method

❶ Preheat the grill. Rinse the salmon steaks under cold running water, pat dry with paper towels and place in a large, shallow, nonmetallic dish. Sprinkle with the lime rind and pour the juice over them. Season to taste with salt and pepper, cover, and leave to stand while you make the salsa.

❷ Place the mango flesh in a bowl with the onion. Cut the passion fruit in half and scoop out the seeds and the pulp with a teaspoon. Add to the bowl. Tear the basil leaves and add them to the bowl with the lime juice. Season to taste with salt and stir well. Cover with plastic wrap and reserve until required.

❸ Cook the salmon steaks over medium-hot coals for 3–4 minutes on each side. Serve immediately with the salsa.

Stuffed Sardines

Grilled fresh sardines are always a popular choice. They are usually just plainly grilled, but here they are stuffed with herbs and coated in a mild spice mixture.

serves 6

¼ cup fresh parsley, finely chopped	⅔ cup all-purpose flour
4 garlic cloves, finely chopped	1 tsp ground cumin
12 fresh sardines, cleaned and scaled	salt and pepper
3 tbsp lemon juice	olive oil, for brushing

Method

❶ Place the parsley and garlic in a bowl and mix together. Rinse the fish inside and out under cold running water and pat dry with paper towels. Spoon the herb mixture into the fish cavities and pat the remainder all over the outside of the fish. Sprinkle the sardines with lemon juice and transfer to a large, shallow, nonmetallic dish. Cover with plastic wrap and leave to marinate in the refrigerator for 1 hour.

❷ Preheat the grill. Mix the flour and ground cumin together in a bowl, then season to taste with salt and pepper. Spread out the seasoned flour on a large plate and gently roll the sardines in the flour to coat.

❸ Brush the sardines with olive oil and cook over medium-hot coals for 3–4 minutes on each side. Serve immediately.

Orange & Lemon Peppered Angler Fish

Although angler fish appears quite expensive, there is very little wastage as, apart from the central backbone, the entire tail is edible. Its flavor is meaty and succulent.

serves 6

2 oranges

2 lemons

2 angler fish tails, about 1 lb 2 oz/500 g
each, skinned and cut into 4 fillets

6 fresh lemon thyme sprigs

2 tbsp olive oil

salt

2 tbsp green peppercorns,
lightly crushed

To garnish

orange wedges

lemon wedges

Method

❶ Cut 8 orange slices and 8 lemon slices, reserving the remaining fruit. Rinse the angler fish fillets under cold running water and pat dry with paper towels. Place 1 fillet from each fish tail, cut side up, on a counter and divide the citrus slices between them. Top with the lemon thyme. Reassemble the tails and tie them securely together at intervals with kitchen string or trussing thread. Place the tails in a large, shallow, nonmetallic dish.

❷ Squeeze the juice from the remaining fruit and mix with the olive oil in a pitcher. Season to taste with salt, then spoon the mixture over the fish. Cover with plastic wrap and leave to marinate in the refrigerator for up to 1 hour, spooning the marinade over the fish tails once or twice.

❸ Preheat the grill. Drain the fish tails, reserving the marinade. Sprinkle the crushed green peppercorns over the fish, pressing them in with your fingers. Cook the fish over medium-hot coals, turning and brushing frequently with the reserved marinade, for 20–25 minutes. Transfer to a cutting board, remove and discard the string, and cut the fish tails into slices. Serve immediately, garnished with orange and lemon wedges.

Bacon-Wrapped Trout

This classic, pan-fried combination is even more delicious cooked on the grill, as the smoky flavor of the bacon becomes more pronounced in contrast to the delicate flesh of the fish.

serves 4

4 trout, cleaned

4 strips bacon

4 tbsp all-purpose flour

salt and pepper

2 tbsp olive oil

2 tbsp lemon juice

corn salad, to serve

To garnish

fresh parsley sprigs

lemon wedges

Method

❶ Preheat the grill. Rinse the trout inside and out under cold running water and pat dry with paper towels. Cut off any rind and stretch the bacon using the back of a heavy, flat-bladed knife.

❷ Season the flour with salt and pepper and spread it out on a large, flat plate. Gently roll each trout in the seasoned flour until thoroughly coated. Beginning just below the head, wrap a strip of bacon in a spiral along the length of each fish.

❸ Brush the trout with olive oil and cook over medium-hot coals for 5–8 minutes on each side. Transfer to 4 large serving plates and drizzle with the lemon juice. Garnish with parsley and lemon wedges and serve with corn salad.

Sizzling Scallops

This is a new and great way to cook scallops on the grill. You can also use other shellfish, such as oysters, if you prefer.

serves 4

1 lemon	2 cups fresh whole-wheat bread crumbs
6 tbsp olive oil	4 tbsp butter, melted
salt and pepper	lemon wedges, to garnish (optional)
12 prepared scallops	

Method

❶ Finely grate the lemon rind, then place it in a dish with the olive oil and mix together. Season to taste. Add the scallops, tossing to coat, then cover and leave to marinate for 30 minutes.

❷ Preheat the barbecue. Place the bread crumbs in a large bowl. Add the scallops, one at a time, and toss until they are well coated, then thread on to individual presoaked wooden skewers. Drizzle with the melted butter.

❸ Cook the breaded scallops over medium-hot coals, turning once, for 8–10 minutes. Transfer to a large serving dish, garnish with lemon wedges, if you like, and serve immediately.

Chargrilled Devils

This is a barbecue version of the classic appetizer "angels on horseback," and goes to prove how sophisticated and elegant alfresco dining can be.

serves 4

36 fresh oysters

18 strips bacon

1 tbsp mild paprika

1 tsp cayenne pepper

Sauce

1 fresh red chile, seeded and finely chopped

1 garlic clove, finely chopped

1 shallot, finely chopped

2 tbsp finely chopped fresh parsley

2 tbsp lemon juice

salt and pepper

Method

❶ Preheat the grill. Open the oysters, catching the juice from the shells in a bowl. Cut the oysters from the bottom shells, reserve, and tip any remaining juice into the bowl. To make the sauce, add the red chile, garlic, shallot, parsley, and lemon juice to the bowl, then season to taste with salt and pepper and mix well. Cover the bowl with plastic wrap and leave to chill in the refrigerator until required.

❷ Remove any rind and cut each bacon strip in half across the center. Season the oysters with paprika and cayenne, then roll each one up in half a bacon strip. Spear each wrapped oyster with a presoaked wooden toothpick or thread 9 on to each of 4 presoaked wooden skewers.

❸ Cook over hot coals, turning frequently, for 5 minutes, or until the bacon is well browned and crispy. Transfer to a large serving plate and serve immediately with the sauce.

Variation

You can replace the shallot with a small, finely chopped onion and the fresh parsley with the same amount of snipped fresh chives, if you prefer.

Spanish Shrimp

**These fresh shrimp are served with a fiery tomato and chili sauce.
If you prefer a milder flavor, you can reduce the number of chiles.**

serves 6

1 bunch of fresh flat-leaf parsley

36 large, raw shrimp, peeled, with tails
left on, and deveined

3–4 tbsp olive oil

lemon wedges, to garnish

Sauce

6 fresh red chiles

1 onion, chopped

2 garlic cloves, chopped

1 lb/450 g tomatoes, chopped

3 tbsp olive oil

pinch of sugar

salt and pepper

Method

❶ Preheat the grill. Chop enough parsley to fill 2 tablespoons and reserve. To make the sauce, seed and chop the chiles, then put into a food processor with the onion and garlic and process until finely chopped. Add the tomatoes and olive oil and process to a purée.

❷ Transfer the mixture to a pan set over a very low heat, stir in the sugar, and season to taste with salt and pepper. Simmer very gently, without boiling, for 15 minutes. Transfer the sauce to an earthenware bowl and place on the side of the grill to keep warm.

❸ Rinse the shrimp under cold running water and pat dry on paper towels. Mix the parsley and olive oil in a dish, add the shrimp, and toss well to coat. Cook the shrimp over medium-hot coals for 3 minutes on each side, or until they have changed color. Transfer to a plate, garnish with lemon wedges, and serve with the sauce.

Vegetables
& Salads

Stuffed Tomato Pockets

An unusual filling for stuffed tomatoes, the spinach and cheese are given extra flavor with toasted sunflower seeds.

serves 4

1 tbsp olive oil	pinch of freshly grated nutmeg
2 tbsp sunflower seeds	salt and pepper
1 onion, finely chopped	4 beef tomatoes
1 garlic clove, finely chopped	5 oz/140 g mozzarella cheese, diced
1 lb/450 g fresh spinach, thick stalks removed and leaves shredded	

Method

❶ Preheat the grill. Heat the oil in a heavy-based pan. Add the sunflower seeds and cook, stirring constantly, for 2 minutes, or until golden. Add the onion and cook over a low heat, stirring occasionally, for 5 minutes, or until softened but not browned. Add the garlic and spinach, cover, and cook for 2–3 minutes, or until the spinach has wilted. Remove the pan from the heat and season to taste with nutmeg, salt, and pepper. Leave to cool.

❷ Using a sharp knife, cut off and reserve a thin slice from the top of each tomato and scoop out the flesh with a teaspoon, taking care not to pierce the shell. Chop the flesh and stir it into the spinach mixture with the mozzarella cheese.

❸ Fill the tomato shells with the spinach and cheese mixture and replace the tops. Cut 4 squares of foil, each large enough to enclose a tomato. Place one tomato in the center of each square and fold up the sides to enclose securely. Cook over hot coals, turning occasionally, for 10 minutes. Serve immediately in the parcels.

Potato Fans

These garlic-flavored roast potatoes make a wonderful alternative to baked potatoes. Allow plenty of time for cooking.

serves 6

6 large potatoes, scrubbed but
not peeled

2 tbsp garlic-flavored olive oil

Method

❶ Preheat the grill. Using a sharp knife, make a series of cuts across the potatoes almost all the way through. Cut out 6 squares of foil, each large enough to enclose a potato.

❷ Place a potato on each square of foil and brush generously with the garlic-flavored oil. Fold up the sides of the foil to enclose the potatoes completely.

❸ Cook over hot coals, turning occasionally, for 1 hour. To serve, open the foil parcels and gently pinch the potatoes to open up the fans.

Zucchini & Cheese Pockets

These delicately flavored, melt-in-the-mouth stuffed zucchini are ideal if you are serving food to both meat-eaters and vegetarians, as the pockets can be cooked in the grill embers and so avoid any contact with meat on the grill.

serves 8

1 small bunch of fresh mint

8 zucchini

1 tbsp olive oil, plus extra for brushing

4 oz/115 g feta cheese, cut into strips

pepper

Method

❶ Preheat the grill. Using a sharp knife, finely chop enough mint to fill 1 tablespoon. Reserve until required. Cut out 8 rectangles of foil, each large enough to enclose a zucchini, and brush lightly with olive oil. Cut a slit along the length of each zucchini and place them on the foil rectangles.

❷ Insert strips of feta cheese along the slits in the zucchini, then drizzle the olive oil over the top, sprinkle with the reserved chopped mint, and season to taste with pepper. Fold in the sides of the foil and seal the edges securely to enclose the cheese-stuffed zucchini completely.

❸ Bake the zucchini pockets in the grill embers for 30 minutes. Carefully unwrap the pockets and serve immediately.

Variation

If you like, substitute mozzarella or fontina cheese for the feta cheese and replace the mint with the same amount of fresh parsley.

Vegetarian Brochettes

The great thing about tofu—apart from the fact that it is packed
with protein—is its ability to absorb other flavors, in this case
a mustard and honey flavored glaze.

serves 4

2 zucchini

1 yellow bell pepper, seeded
and quartered

8 oz/225 g firm tofu (drained weight)

4 cherry tomatoes

4 pearl onions

8 white mushrooms

Honey glaze

2 tbsp olive oil

1 tbsp Meaux or Dijon mustard

1 tbsp clear honey

salt and pepper

Method

❶ Preheat the grill. Using a vegetable peeler, peel off strips of skin along the length of the zucchini to leave alternate yellow and green stripes, then cut each zucchini into 8 thick slices. Cut each of the yellow bell pepper quarters in half. Cut the drained tofu into 1-inch/2.5-cm cubes.

❷ Thread the pieces of bell pepper, zucchini slices, tofu cubes, cherry tomatoes, pearl onions, and white mushrooms on to 4 flat metal skewers. To make the glaze, mix the olive oil, mustard, and honey together in a pitcher and season to taste with salt and pepper.

❸ Brush the brochettes with the honey glaze and cook over medium-hot coals, turning and brushing frequently with the glaze, for 8–10 minutes. Serve.

Variation

You can also make vegetable brochettes. Omit the tofu and use eggplant chunks, zucchini chunks, and small strips of red bell pepper.

Summer Vegetable Pockets

You can use any baby vegetables you like—pattypan squash, corn cobs, and plum tomatoes look attractive and add color. Serve with grilled meat or fish for a substantial barbecue main course.

serves 4

2 lb 4 oz/1 kg mixed baby vegetables, such as carrots, pattypan squash, corn cobs, plum tomatoes, leeks, zucchini, and onions

1 lemon

4 oz/115 g unsalted butter

3 tbsp chopped mixed fresh herbs, such as parsley, thyme, and chervil

2 garlic cloves

salt and pepper

Method

❶ Preheat the grill. Cut out 4 x 12-inch/ 30-cm squares of foil and divide the vegetables equally between them.

❷ Using a grater, finely grate the lemon rind, then squeeze the juice from the lemon and reserve until required. Put the lemon rind, butter, herbs, and garlic into a food processor and process until blended, then season to taste with salt and pepper. Alternatively, beat together in a bowl until blended.

❸ Divide the flavored butter equally between the vegetables, dotting it on top. Fold up the sides of the foil to enclose the vegetables, sealing securely. Cook over medium-hot coals, turning occasionally, for 25–30 minutes. Open the pockets, sprinkle with the reserved lemon juice, and serve immediately.

Variation

If baby vegetables are unavailable, then use larger vegetables cut into small pieces, such as thin sticks of zucchini and carrot, and eggplant chunks.

Corn-on-the-Cob with Blue Cheese Dressing

Corn cobs are delicious grilled over charcoal. Cook them as soon after purchase as possible because they quickly lose their sweetness as their natural sugars convert to starch.

serves 6

5 oz/140 g Danish Blue cheese

5 oz/140 g curd cheese

½ cup natural Greek yogurt

salt and pepper

6 corn cobs in their husks

Method

❶ Preheat the grill. Crumble the Danish Blue cheese, then place in a bowl. Beat with a wooden spoon until creamy. Beat in the curd cheese until thoroughly blended. Gradually beat in the yogurt and season to taste with salt and pepper. Cover with plastic wrap and leave to chill in the refrigerator until required.

❷ Fold back the husks on each corn cob and remove the silks. Smooth the husks back into place. Cut out 6 rectangles of foil, each large enough to enclose a corn cob. Wrap the corn cobs in the foil.

❸ Cook the corn cobs over hot coals, turning frequently, for 15–20 minutes. Unwrap the corn cobs and discard the foil. Peel back the husk on one side of each and trim off with a sharp knife or kitchen scissors. Serve immediately with the blue cheese dressing.

Cajun Vegetables

These spicy vegetables would be a perfect accompaniment to some colorful Caribbean Fish Kabobs (see page 44).

serves 4

4 corn cobs

2 sweet potatoes, scrubbed but not peeled

2 tbsp butter, melted

Spice mix

2 tsp paprika

1 tsp ground cumin

1 tsp ground coriander

1 tsp ground black pepper

$\frac{1}{2}$–1 tsp chili powder

Method

❶ Preheat the grill. To make the spice mix, mix all the ingredients together in a small bowl.

❷ Remove the husks and silks from the corn cobs, then cut each cob into 4 equal chunks. Cut the sweet potatoes into thick slices, but do not peel. Brush the corn chunks and sweet potato slices with melted butter and sprinkle with some spice mix.

❸ Cook the corn cobs and sweet potatoes over medium-hot coals, turning frequently, for 12–15 minutes. Brush with more melted butter and sprinkle with extra spice mixture during cooking. Transfer the corn and sweet potatoes to a large serving plate and serve immediately.

Prune, Apricot & Onion Skewers

These flavorsome, fruity skewers would go well with plain grilled pork chops, duck breasts, lamb steaks, or kabobs, as their sweetness would counteract the richness of the meat.

serves 4

1 lb/450 g pearl onions

6 oz/175 g prunes, pitted

8 oz/225 g dried apricots, pitted

2-inch/5-cm cinnamon stick

1 cup white wine

2 tbsp chili sauce

2 tbsp sunflower oil

Method

❶ Cut the tops off the onions and peel off the skin. Reserve until required. Place the prunes, apricots, cinnamon, and wine in a heavy-based pan and bring to a boil. Reduce the heat and simmer for 5 minutes. Drain, reserving the cooking liquid and cinnamon, and leave the fruit until cool enough to handle.

❷ Return the cooking liquid and cinnamon stick to the pan, return to a boil, and boil until reduced by half. Remove the pan from the heat and remove and discard the cinnamon stick. Stir in the chili sauce and oil.

❸ Thread the prunes, apricots, and onions on to several flat metal skewers. Cook over medium-hot coals, turning and brushing frequently with the wine mixture, for 10 minutes. Serve immediately.

Eggplant
with Tsatziki

This makes a delicious appetizer for a barbecue party or can be served as part of a vegetarian barbecue meze with Stuffed Tomato Pockets (see page 62), or Zucchini & Cheese Pockets (see page 66).

serves 4

2 tbsp olive oil	Tsatziki
salt and pepper	½ cucumber
2 eggplants, thinly sliced	¾ cup natural Greek yogurt
	4 scallions, finely sliced
	1 garlic clove, finely chopped
	3 tbsp chopped fresh mint
	salt and pepper
	1 fresh mint sprig, to garnish

Method

❶ Preheat the grill. To make the tsatziki, finely chop the cucumber. Place the yogurt in a bowl and beat well until smooth. Stir in the cucumber, scallions, garlic, and mint until distributed evenly through the yogurt. Season to taste with salt and pepper. Transfer to a serving bowl, cover with plastic wrap, and leave to chill in the refrigerator until required.

❷ Season the olive oil with salt and pepper, then brush the eggplant slices with the oil.

❸ Cook the eggplant over hot coals for 5 minutes on each side, brushing with more oil, if necessary. Transfer to a large serving plate and serve immediately with the tsatziki, garnished with a mint sprig.

Tropical Rice Salad

Rice salads are always popular and this colorful, fruity mixture goes especially well with barbecued meat or chicken.

serves 4

generous ½ cup long-grain rice

salt and pepper

4 scallions

8 oz/225 g canned pineapple pieces in natural juice

1 cup canned corn, drained

2 red bell peppers, seeded and diced

3 tbsp golden raisins

Dressing

1 tbsp groundnut oil

1 tbsp hazelnut oil

1 tbsp light soy sauce

1 garlic clove, finely chopped

1 tsp chopped fresh gingerroot

Method

❶ Cook the rice in a large pan of lightly salted boiling water for 15 minutes, or until tender. Drain thoroughly and rinse under cold running water. Place the rice in a large serving bowl.

❷ Using a sharp knife, finely slice the scallions. Drain the pineapple pieces, reserving the juice in a pitcher. Add the pineapple pieces, corn, red bell peppers, sliced scallions, and golden raisins to the rice and mix lightly.

❸ Add all the dressing ingredients to the reserved pineapple juice, whisking well, and season to taste with salt and pepper. Pour the dressing over the salad and toss until the salad is thoroughly coated. Serve immediately.

Variation

Try other flavored nut oils, such as walnut oil or sesame oil. You can also substitute sunflower oil for the groundnut oil, if you prefer.

Tabbouleh

This Middle Eastern salad is increasingly fashionable. It is a classic accompaniment for lamb, but goes well with most grilled meat.

serves 4

¾ cup bulgur wheat

3 tbsp extra virgin olive oil

4 tbsp lemon juice

salt and pepper

4 scallions

1 green bell pepper, seeded and sliced

4 tomatoes, chopped

2 tbsp chopped fresh parsley

2 tbsp chopped fresh mint

8 black olives, pitted

fresh mint sprigs, to garnish

Method

❶ Place the bulgur wheat in a large bowl and add enough cold water to cover. Leave to stand for 30 minutes, or until the wheat has doubled in size. Drain well and press out as much liquid as possible. Spread out the wheat on paper towels to dry.

❷ Place the wheat in a serving bowl. Mix the olive oil and lemon juice together in a pitcher and season to taste with salt and pepper. Pour the lemon mixture over the wheat and leave to marinate for 1 hour.

❸ Using a sharp knife, finely slice the scallions, then add to the salad with the green bell pepper, tomatoes, parsley, and mint and toss lightly to mix. Top the salad with the olives and garnish with fresh mint sprigs, then serve.

Variation

Use different types of fresh tomatoes—try vine-ripened tomatoes, which have a delicate, sweet flavor, or cherry tomatoes, cut in half.

Cheese & Walnut Pasta Salad

This is an ideal salad to serve with a barbecue, as it is not just a pasta salad, which can seem a little mundane, but also includes a colorful mix of crisp salad greens.

serves 4

3½ cups dried fusilli	4 oz/115 g walnut halves
salt and pepper	4 tbsp sunflower oil
8 oz/225 g dolcelatte cheese	2 tbsp walnut oil
3½ oz/100 g mixed salad greens, such	2 tbsp red wine vinegar
as oak leaf lettuce, radicchio, baby spinach,	
arugula, and corn salad	

Method

❶ Cook the pasta in a large pan of lightly salted boiling water for 8–10 minutes, or until tender, but still firm to the bite. Drain, rinse under cold running water, and drain again.

❷ Using a sharp knife, cut the dolcelatte cheese into cubes. Place the salad greens in a large serving bowl and add the cooked pasta. Sprinkle the dolcelatte cheese on top.

❸ Preheat the broiler to medium. Place the walnut halves on a large baking tray and cook under the broiler for a few minutes, or until lightly toasted. Leave to cool. Mix the sunflower oil, walnut oil, and red wine vinegar together in a pitcher and season to taste with salt and pepper. Pour the dressing over the salad, toss lightly, then top with the toasted walnuts.

Red & Green Salad

Beet and orange is a classic combination and here they are mixed with tender baby spinach leaves to make a dramatic and colorful warm salad.

serves 4

1 lb 7 oz/650 g cooked beets, peeled

3 tbsp extra virgin olive oil

juice of 1 orange

1 tsp superfine sugar

1 tsp fennel seeds

salt and pepper

4 oz/115 g fresh baby spinach leaves

Method

❶ Using a sharp knife, dice the cooked beet and reserve until required. Heat the olive oil in a small, heavy-based pan. Add the orange juice, sugar, and fennel seeds and season to taste with salt and pepper. Stir constantly until the sugar has dissolved.

❷ Add the reserved beets to the pan and stir gently to coat. Remove the pan from the heat.

❸ Arrange the baby spinach leaves in a large salad bowl. Spoon the warmed beets on top and serve immediately.

Desserts

Mixed Fruit Kabobs

You can use almost any firm-fleshed fruit to make these colorful,
quick and easy kabobs. Remember to soak the wooden skewers in cold water
before using to prevent burning.

serves 4

2 nectarines, halved and pitted

2 kiwi fruit

4 red plums

1 mango, peeled, halved and pitted

2 bananas, peeled and thickly sliced

8 strawberries, hulled

1 tbsp clear honey

3 tbsp Cointreau

Method

❶ Cut the nectarine halves in half again and place in a large, shallow dish. Peel and quarter the kiwi fruit. Cut the plums in half and remove the stones. Cut the mango flesh into chunks and add to the dish with the kiwi fruit, plums, bananas, and strawberries.

❷ Mix the honey and Cointreau together in a pitcher until well blended. Pour the mixture over the fruit and toss lightly to coat. Cover with plastic wrap and leave to marinate in the refrigerator for 1 hour.

❸ Preheat the grill. Drain the fruit, reserving the marinade. Thread the fruit on to several presoaked wooden skewers and cook over medium-hot coals, turning and brushing frequently with the reserved marinade, for 5–7 minutes, then serve.

Barbecued Baked Apples

When they are wrapped in kitchen foil, apples bake to perfection on the grill and make a delightful finale to any meal.

serves 4

4 medium cooking apples

¼ cup walnuts, chopped

⅓ cup ground almonds

¼ cup light muscovado sugar

5–6 cherries, chopped

2 x 1-inch/2.5-cm pieces stem ginger, chopped

1 tbsp Amaretto (optional)

4 tbsp butter

whipping cream or natural yogurt, to serve

Method

❶ Core the apples and, using a sharp knife, score each one around the middle to prevent the apple skins from splitting while cooking on the grill.

❷ To make the filling, chop the stem ginger pieces and mix together with the walnuts, almonds, sugar, cherries, and Amaretto, if using, in a small bowl.

❸ Spoon some filling mixture into each apple, pushing it down into the hollowed-out core. Mound a little of the filling mixture on top of each apple.

❹ Place each apple on a large square of double thickness foil and generously dot all over with the butter. Gather up and seal the foil so that the filled apple is completely enclosed.

❺ Grill the foil pockets containing the apples over hot coals for 25–30 minutes or until tender.

❻ Transfer the apples to warm, individual serving plates. Serve with lashings of whipped cream or thick natural yogurt.

Variation

If the coals are dying down, place the foil pockets directly on to the coals, raking them up around the apples. Grill for 25–30 minutes and serve with whipped cream or natural yogurt.

Banana Sizzles

Bananas are particularly sweet and delicious when grilled—
and conveniently come with their own protective wrapping.

serves 4

3 tbsp butter, softened

2 tbsp dark rum

1 tbsp orange juice

4 tbsp dark muscovado sugar

pinch of ground cinnamon

4 bananas

orange zest, to decorate

Method

❶ Preheat the grill. Beat the butter with the rum, orange juice, sugar, and cinnamon in a small bowl until thoroughly blended and smooth.

❷ Place the bananas, without peeling, over hot coals and cook, turning frequently, for 6–8 minutes, or until the skins are blackened.

❸ Transfer the bananas to serving plates, slit the skins, and cut partially through the flesh lengthwise. Divide the flavored butter between the bananas, decorate with orange zest, and serve.

Recipe List

- Bacon Koftas *26* • Bacon-Wrapped Trout *52* • Banana Sizzles *94*

- Barbecued Baked Apples *92* • Best Ever Burgers *12* • Cajun Vegetables *74*

- Caribbean Fish Kabobs *44* • Chargrilled Devils *56* • Cheese & Walnut Pasta Salad *84*

- Corn-on-the-Cob with Blue Cheese Dressing *72* • Eggplant with Tsatziki *78*

- Fabulous Frankfurter Skewers *28* • Fruity Duck *40* • Hot Red Chicken *34*

- Luxury Cheeseburgers *14* • Meatballs on Sticks *24* • Minted Lamb Steaks *18*

- Mixed Fruit Kabobs *90* • Mustard & Honey Drumsticks *30*

- Normandy Brochettes *20* • Orange & Lemon Peppered Angler Fish *50*

- Potato Fans *64* • Prune, Apricot & Onion Skewers *76* • Rack & Ruin *16*

- Red & Green Salad *86* • Sage & Lemon Squab Chickens *32*

- Salmon with Mango Salsa *46* • Sausages with Barbecue Sauce *22*

- Sizzling Scallops *54* • Spanish Shrimp *58* • Stuffed Sardines *48*

- Stuffed Tomato Pockets *62* • Summer Vegetable Pockets *70*

- Tabasco Steaks with Parsley Butter *10* • Tabbouleh *82* • Tarragon Turkey *38*

- Tropical Rice Salad *80* • Turkey Rolls *36* • Vegetarian Brochettes *68*

- Zucchini & Cheese Pockets *66*